A to Z of

Winter

Tracy Nelson Maurer

Rourke
Publishing LLC
Vero Beach, Florida 32964

www.rourkepublishing.com

PHOTO CREDITS: All photos © Micheal Maurer except: Cover © EyeWire; pages 8, 11, 12, 13, 30 © Lois M. Nelson; page 17 © Diane Farleo; pages 9, 25 © Tracy M. Maurer; pages 20, 23, 27 © Lynn M. Stone; page 22 courtesy of *Outdoor Oklahoma*, Oklahoma Department of Wildlife Conservation

Cover photo: *Winter brings snow and sledding fun.*

Editor: Frank Sloan

Cover and page design by Nicola Stratford

About the Author:

Tracy Nelson Maurer specializes in nonfiction and business writing. Her most recently published children's books include the *RadSports* series, also from Rourke Publishing LLC. A graduate of the University of Minnesota Journalism School, Tracy lives with her husband Mike and two children in Superior, Wisconsin.

Acknowledgments:
The author extends heartfelt appreciation to the children, parents, teachers, and photographers who graciously participated in this project. Your enthusiasm made every season special!

Library of Congress Cataloging-in-Publication Data

Maurer, Tracy, 1965-
  Winter / Tracy Nelson Maurer.
      p. cm. — (A to Z of seasons)
Summary: Illustrations and simple text present a variety of things seen in the winter.
  ISBN 1-58952-199-4 (hardcover)
  1. Winter—Juvenile literature. [1. Winter. 2. Alphabet.] I. Title.
  QB637.8 .M38 2002
  428.1--dc21

                                                          2002004343

Printed in the USA

w/w

WINTER

Do you live where it snows in the winter? Many places and things, or nouns, look very different in this cold season. From A to Z, winter wonders are everywhere. Can you think of other winter nouns?

Aa

Angels are fun to make.

Bb

Boats wait in ice for spring.

Cc

Chickadees eat seeds.

Dd

Drifts cover the walk.

Ee

Evergreens look pretty.

Ff

Frost clouds the windows.

10

Gg

Goggles guard eyes.

Hh

Hats protect ears.

Ice fills the harbor.

Jj

Jackets feel cozy.

Kids play in the snow.

Lakes freeze solid.

16

Mm

Mittens keep hands warm.

Nn

Nature trails are covered in snow.

Owls hunt at night.

20

Pp

Plows clear the roads.

Quail peck for food.

Rr

Rabbits may turn white.

Ss

Sleds rush downhill.

Tt

Tracks mark the snow.

Uu

Underwear is the first layer.

Vv

Vixen, or fox, sniff for food.

27

Ww

Wreaths decorate fences.

28

Xx

X-ing signs warn drivers.

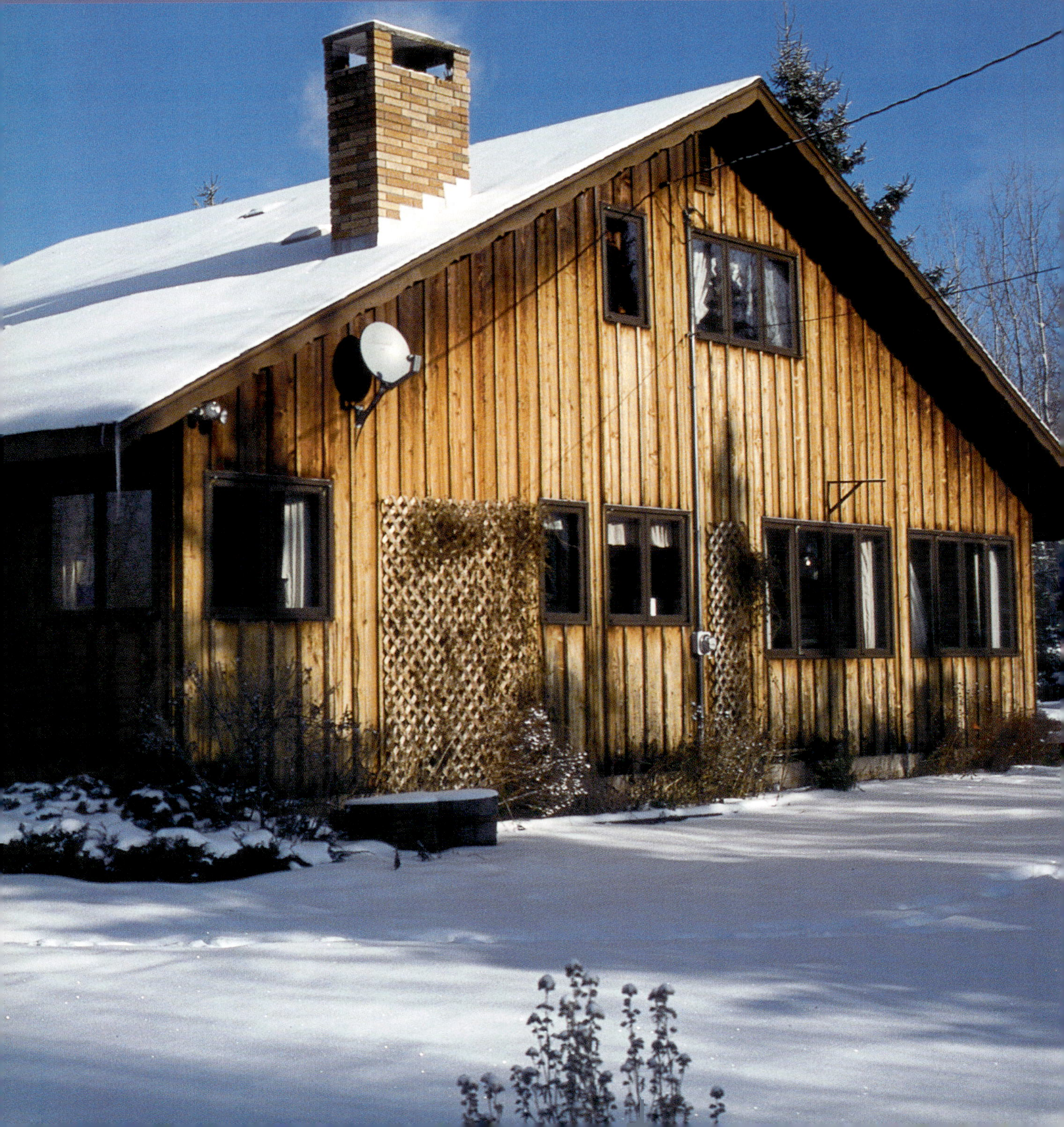

Yy

Yards lie under the snow.

Zz

Zero degrees Celsius freezes water.